Ocean Eyes, Starry Skies

What you're not changing, you're choosing.

Ishwariya Gopi

BookLeaf Publishing

India | USA | UK

Made with ❤ on the BookLeaf Publishing Platform
www.bookleafpub.in
www.bookleafpub.com

Dedication

To every believer

Preface

Inspired by nature in all aspects. I travel to meet people from different cultures. On one such visit, I created the characters in this book; that's where the magic began.

Most of us are chasing dreams, but what dreams? At what cost? Falling is easy, staying is love. This book is a poetic conversation of fictional characters as they fall in love, hoping to stay together until eternity.

The idea of love is an amazing compilation of emotions experienced by people from different cultural backgrounds, despite the differences, they face all challenges just to bring life to their feelings for one another.

We go so far for numerous things that don't even matter. How far can one go for love?

Acknowledgements

There's something strangely beautiful about writing a second book, it's a return, a reckoning, a quiet conversation with self when I began the first one.

When I released *Few Days of Cute Cringe*, I was unsure, honest, messy, and maybe a little terrified. It was fictional, yes, but it carried truths in disguise. So does this one.

To everyone who picked up my first book and let it live in your tote bags, bookshelves, or browser tabs, thank you. Your unexpected love gave me the space and courage to continue weaving more stories into verse. You helped me believe that the softest voices can still echo.

This second book is different. The words came slower, the emotions sharper. The characters, louder. Fictional poetry has always been a delicate balance for me, one foot in imagination, the other knee-deep in memory. To all the almosts, what-ifs, and never-will-bes that inspired these pages, you were fiction, but you felt real enough to ache.

To those who listened when I read drafts aloud at odd hours, over crackly voice notes, or in the coffee-stained journal, thank you. Your silence and your sighs said more than any critique ever could.

To my mom, you loved me through every creative meltdown, every self-imposed deadline, every "does this even make sense?" moment. Thank you for reminding me that even when I doubted the work, the work never really left me.

To the version of me who almost didn't write this one, I'm glad you did. I'm glad you stayed. I'm glad you trusted the silence enough to fill it with poetry again.

To the poets and storytellers who came before me, who made language feel like home, thank you for showing me what it means to be tender with words and ruthless with truth.

And to you, the reader holding this book, I'm grateful. Fictional poetry is a strange little genre to fall in love with, but here we are, you and I, meeting somewhere between a poem and a possibility.

This book is not a sequel, it's a sibling. A little less shy, a little more daring, and just as full of feeling.

Thank you for reading. Thank you for feeling.

With love, ink, and a lot of almost-truths,
Ishwariya Gopi

Ocean eyes

Fire to my soul,
Light to my life,
Route to my heart,
My Ocean Eyes!

Don't ask me again,
what you mean to me.
I've given my answer,
My Ocean Eyes!

Tiny flower

When I held your hand, I knew it.
That we're going to keep this forever.
Then one day, you chose to seal my thoughts with that
little flower.
I know you'd think you're the lucky one here.
But in reality, I'm the one who finally found my long-lost
lover.

Park Bench

Morning walks, random talks,
we sat on a park bench together.
I turned to look at her,
She was already looking at me.
My heart felt light as a feather.
I looked around and sat closer to her,
she held my hand and smiled.
I could feel the tension of awkward silence,
The scent of her aura is wild!

Meadows of love

Amongst all the people in the ride,
My eyes look for you.
Though you're not in the mood for the vibe,
You read my eyes and take a seat.
You sat right beside me and looked me in the eye.
That smile on your face conveys a lot.
Do you mean, you're here for me?
Do you mean, you'd do things out of your lane to keep
me company?
Do you mean, I'd never have to see the world alone?
A million questions in my mind, filling the void.
Suddenly, the vehicle stops at the meadow.
You de-board before me and kneel,
offering to help me take off my footwear.
How do I explain what I feel?

A Sweet Sail

Last sail for the day, and we're already late for it.
He occupies the middle seat, and by his side I sit,
the darker it grows as we're nearing dusk.
At the cinnamon island, we relax and smell its husk.
He holds hands as we walk towards our ferry,
We take pictures together, though it is dark and blurry.
I know this is surreal, I wish it would stay longer.
I know this is a mirage, I wish we could be stronger

Night under the Moon

We've been drinking, she is drunk.
Under the influence, she dresses up like a punk.
She leans on my shoulder and asks for a beach date.
I know for a fact she's going to regret this once she can
stand straight.
However, I take her to the beach,
She keeps talking like it's the end of the world.
I keep nodding to all her talks,
cause she is my five-foot world.
Through the night, we look at the moon, looking at us.
Thinking of where I come from, will there ever be an
"us"?

Life with You

I wish, I wish, a life with you.
I've said it a million times, I'll say it more, too.
I see a future in the hope we share,
every instance, every challenge, I dare.
Does love come with conditions?
Does love come with a manual?
All I know, it happens when it happens.
Is it sinful to be in love?
If yes, you may call me a sinner, I don't mind.
for I know I'm deeply in love.
All I wish is a life with you!
and I know you wish that too.

City Lights

Shiny light, shining bright, all over the streets,
We're hopping from shop to shop,
wondering what to eat.
distracted by the lanterns,
I stop by to give a glance.
He stands with me, patiently,
Isn't this subtle romance?
He points at the restaurant on the other side of the road,
I smile and nod, yes.
We take a table, and I begin my casual rant,
Cause he listens and speaks less.
We sit there for hours, and when it's time to leave,
We realize it's too late.
We step out to the rescue of the city lights,
Shiny light, shining bright, all over the streets,

Rythm

The music note I share,
It shows a bit of despair,
The language barrier we have,
I look up the lyrics too.
I share the track for you to enjoy.
you insist I share its meaning too.
The meaning speaks all I wish I could,
but will you judge me? cause I love you.
By the way you behave, I see it in your eyes,
with all the cultural difference we have,
I'm just trying not to hurt you.
Let's just live the rhythm, the moment we have!
Now my head is all blue!

Cafe date

Coffee for him, green tea for her,
just like their tastes, abstract, they were.
He tries to sit by her side,
but does not succeed.
She keeps her bag next to her,
sits facing him,
Their eyes lock as they speak,
She hates coffee, and he hates green tea,
when they realize this, the ask together,
How are you even attracted to me?

Birthday Surprise

I cross the ocean to hold her hand,
I buy a bunch of flowers,
I wait for hours on the plane,
To see my pretty lover,
I wonder what she has planned.
I hope I don't ruin the surprise.
I land at her native airport,
and pick up some souvenirs for her,
I'm walking with a lot of things on my mind,
Should I buy a cake too?
As I walk towards the exit, she waits,
I wonder how she knew.
She laughed at me as I was surprised,
I remembered, she has access to my emails too.
Birthday surprise, it was meant to be.
she leaves me surprised, laughing at me.

Mine

You have a sweet name,
It is nice to call,
But, can I call you mine?
This distance between us,
buries me alive.
With you, I feel divine.
Just look at me,
and speak your heart,
Can I call you mine?
I want to take you with me,
and build a home for us,
Will you please be mine?

Scribbles

All the romance is nice and cute,
But the mixed feelings you give!
One moment, you want me there,
Another moment, you want to be here.
Is this some kind of a joke?
It is not funny, feels more like a provoke.
Relationship is hard work, it is not for the weak.
All this time you've been chasing me, feels like hide and
seek.
And all that I write to you, you've been ignoring like
some ripples.
Now I start thinking, love is less poetic and more
scribbles!

Rain

One summer evening,
it rained cats and dogs,
Could I ask the Rain?
The reason for its visit.
Should I act surprised?
This is indeed an unexpected visit.
Is the reason important?
To me, it is.
So, I ask the Rain,
"Why? Rain, Why?"
The Rain replied,
"Even the skies cry!"

Cage and the forest

He is a caged bird, she is from the forest.
Both love to fly and explore the sky.
However, their upbringing differs,
They fall in love and prepare to plan a life together,
forever!
He complains so much about the forest,
She agrees to move into his cage,
He is happy in the cage like he always used to be,
She dies little by little, her forest, she longs to see.
But the cage opens only for feed,
She questions her existence, as well as her need.
One day, she gets her opportunity out of the cage,
Oh no! It's too late, she has forgotten to fly!
She accepts that memory fades with age,
She walks back into the cage with a long sigh!

Chaos

He tells me that he needs me,
acts like he wants me,
Even little emotional acts of his,
Feels like a trigger, taunts me.
Now my mind lies in confusion,
feels like I've been played.
Where do I get my answers from?
For he is mute when I need him the most.
He let me there, frowned in pain,
As his folks stir the roast.
He looks a little like the man I fell for,
Someone I love the most.

Distance

Another state? Another country?
How far for love?
If you have to go, how far would you go?
Family? Pressure?
How far for love?
If you have to go, how far would you go?
Self-respect? Dignity?
How far for love?
If you have to go, how far would you go?
Life? Death?
How far for love?
If you have to go, how far would you go?

Would you even go?

Last hug

Love is not for the weak,
She conveys as they speak,
He listens, but says nothing,
She hopes to hear something.
He cries softly, hugs her air-tight,
He whispers in her ear," I cannot fight."
She breaks down as they speak,
If you cannot fight for us, how can I stay?
He begs for some time, at least another day.
She hugs him tighter as he cries like a baby,
For she knows it is their last hug.
She realizes he's just a baby,
Hoping he'd man up someday.
They part from each other as the flight awaits,
She boards her plane, closes the gates.
Gates to her heart and feelings,
Begging god for rapid healing.

Love, pain, hand in hand

I called her a few times, but she wouldn't answer.
I texted her everywhere, but she wouldn't reply.
She called me a cheater, It doesn't apply.
She knows I love her, she cannot deny.
I know I can fix things, but she doesn't believe.
I don't blame her, I let her perceive.
I was watching helplessly,
As she wept her heart for me,
It was a painful situation,
My cage is toxic, I wouldn't want her to suffer with me.
She belongs to the forest,
That's where she should be.
She knows for a fact, I'm just a helpless lover,
But selfish, I can never be.

Sunset

Sunset is an illusion,
Does the Sun ever set?
If the day dims to you,
Does the Sun really set?
For the Earth goes around the Sun,
The Moon goes around the Earth,
Isn't it beautiful to be as it is?
Rather than reason based on perspectives?
to make your label fit.
If you still believe the sun sets?
Let me tell you something,
Sunset is as subjective as love, it is what it is.

Starry Skies

We wake up together,
Make our tea and start the day,
All silence filled, cold weather,
We check our phones, for strength we pray.
Like this, we spend each and every day,
Our hues are filled with gray.
All this sense of togetherness,
Though separated, we stay.
We share the very same, empty world,
And the starry skies doomsday!
For we share the very same, empty world,
And the starry skies doomsday!